In Loving Memory of a Life Well Lived and a Soul Much

_____

(Loved One)

Birthdate	
Birthplace	
Parents	Mother:
	Father:
Siblings	
Soulmate	
Anniversary	
Children	
Death	Date:
	Time:
	Place:
Funeral Home	
Calling Hours	Date:
	Time:
Funeral	Date:
	Time:
Cemetery	
Burial/Cremation?	

Any other special notes of interest:

_____

_____

_____

_____

YOUR SERVICES:

_____
_____
_____
_____
_____
_____
_____
_____
_____
_____
_____
_____
_____
_____
_____
_____
_____
_____
_____
_____
_____
_____
_____
_____
_____
_____
_____
_____
_____
_____
_____
_____
_____
_____
_____

Obituary and Remembrance Card:

The Day You Died...

My First Night Without You...

I Would Give Anything...

I Never Thought I Could Hurt This Much...

My Most Consistent Feelings Are Those Of...

The Pain And Hurt Is So Unbearable That...

What I Need The Most Is...

Missing You Makes Me...

The Unfairness Of This...

I Feel The Worst...

How Can Anything Ever Be Right Again...

Your Death Has Shook Me To The Core By...

I'm Having The Hardest Time...

Your Words Of Wisdom Would Mean The World To Me Right Now Because...

What Scares Me The Most Is...

I Wish I Would Have...

I Get So Frustrated When...

What Really Pisses Me Off Is...

The Hardest Part Of Losing You And Our Future Is...

I Don't Think I'll Ever Find Someone That...

I Wish I Would Have Told You...

I Wish I Could Hear You Tell Me One More Time That...

I Am Most Grateful For...

When I Think About "Us," I Think...

We Were Perfect Together Because...

WHEN I THINK OF YOU, I THINK OF...

Our Last Great Conversation...

I Loved It When You...

I Loved It When We...

I Wish We Had Gotten The Chance To...

One Of My Favorite Memories...

I Loved The Way You...

You Gave Me...

The Way You Loved Me...

The Things That Instantly Make Me Think Of You...

What Everyone Tells Me You'd Want In This Situation...

What I Feel You'd Want In This Situation...

If I could Do Anything Over One More Time With You...

My Love For You...

If You Can Read These...

I Never Want To Forget...

Who Has Helped Me The Most...

What Has Helped Me The Most...

I Push Myself Forward By...

My Days Without You Are Now Spent...

The Biggest Changes Since You've Been Gone...

What I Really Need To Get Off My Chest...

I May Never Be As Happy As We Were, But I Know You'd Want Me To...

You Made Me A Better Person By...

I Will Always Remember The Way...

My Wishes For Myself Right Now Are...

My Wishes For You Right Now Are...

The Love We Shared...

I Will Honor You And Your Memory By...

When I See You Again...

My 1st Week Without You...

My 2nd Week Without You...

My 3rd Week Without You...

My 1st Month Without You...

My 2nd Month Without You...

My 3rd Month Without You...

My 4th Month Without You...

My 5th Month Without You...

My 6th Month Without You...

My 7th Month Without You...

My 8th Month Without You...

My 9th Month Without You...

My 10th Month Without You...

My 11th Month Without You...

The First Anniversary Of Your Passing...

Made in the USA
Middletown, DE
07 July 2021